A Crow I Know

By Sigal Adler

©**Sigal Adler**

No part of this publication may be reproduced, photocopied, translated, stored in a database or Distributing any form or by any means (electronic, optical or mechanical, including photocopying or recording) without prior written permission of the author.

Publish and printed in USA, 2017

Deep in a garden a special tree grows,

An apple tree owned by a woman named Rose.

She keeps them protected, in every way,

And munches its apples each summer's day.

One sunny day she went to water her trees,

A scorching-hot day with hardly a breeze,

When in flew a mean, screeching feathery brute,

A crow who swooped down and pecked at her fruit.

"That apple is mine!" yelled Rosie in tears,

Waving her hands by that awful crow's ears.

The crow saw her coming and panicked and flew,

Back to the heavens, the mean crow withdrew.

But though Rosie thought at first she was free,

Two days later that crow swooped back to the tree.

Afraid of Rose, who he might chance to meet…

But the fruit was so bright, so tempting, so sweet!

But though Rosie thought at first she was free,

Two days later that crow swooped back to the tree.

Afraid of Rose, who he might chance to meet…

But the fruit was so bright, so tempting, so sweet!

Cheeks red with fury, she shook a long mop,

"He's gone much too far, this time he must stop!"

The crow saw Rosie with rage in her eyes,

Flew back to the heavens in his great surprise.

But Rosie knew then that the crow would come back,

Feared leaving her tree for a snooze or a snack,

The wise crow knew that she couldn't stand guard

So sneaking back in might not be so hard.

That crow had already visited twice,

So Rosie asked Joe, her good friend, for advice.

Joe listened to her and then offered a plan -

Why not build a scarecrow - a big straw-filled man?

Rose thanked Joe for his kind, helpful thought,

"How could he know that – for I sure did not!"

She went out right then to gather supplies,

To build a most fearful bird-scaring surprise.

She first took a mop with a broad-brimmed hat,

Two eyes sewed-on buttons all black, round and flat,

Two fat straw hands stuffed into a shirt

And a pair of old overalls sure wouldn't hurt.

That night, she set out the scarecrow, unseen,

To startle the crow, so cunning and mean.

And heading for home, Rosie giggled with glee,

So certain that crow would turn chicken and flee.

The very next sunrise, just with the first rays,

In swooped the crow, who'd been waiting for days,

To land there and snack on her sweet apple tree…

When suddenly standing there - who should he see?

A new guard, so scary - well, this wasn't good!

He startled and flew off as fast as he could,

From its menacing eyes and broad-brimmed straw hat,

And its face so unpleasant, as fearful as that!

In his terrified panic, the crow lost a feather

While Rose watched indoors, away from the weather.

Then crept to her garden to gobble and taste,

She couldn't let all of that fruit go to waste.

But if you thought crow might give up, you're wrong,

For he realized the guard must go home before long.

What kind of guard, even if he's the best,

Won't quit work or lie down to take a short rest?

So he came a bit later the next day, just in case,

But the guard only stood there in just the same place!

"Oh, no," groaned the crow, and fled fast in fear,

"Does he mean to stand up in this field for a year???"

But one evening, the crow told his wife of the man,

And she understood, as a wise woman can.

She said, "It's a scarecrow, a dummy, not real,"

And boy, what a dummy did she make him feel!

So by morning he came back, knowing no fear,

Along with his wife, who he wished to keep near.

They sat on the scarecrow and pecked his straw head.

"You're just a big dummy!" is what those crows said.

And so the crows sat, chomping every nice fruit,

Till Rose came outside and gave them the boot.

Cheeks bright with fury at those crows' attack

But she had no clue now just how to fight back.

Rose kicked at the dummy, the useless scarecrow,

She said, "You are worthless, and now you must go!"

Pulled out its stake from the hole in the ground

And hid it away where it couldn't be found.

But later that evening, while humming a song,

She had an idea that would help her stand strong.

Though she had failed with her garden's straw man,

At least for tomorrow, she had the best plan.

The next day Rose donned the scarecrow's old clothes,

From broad-brimmed hat down to straw at her toes.

Marched to the field with her hands stuck out straight,

And stood there for what seemed a very long wait.

And just when her neck was unbearably sore,

She heard crows flapping: two wings and then four;

The sneaky black bird and his wife had returned

To steal some more fruit which they hadn't earned.

Boldly, the crows swooped down then and there,

Pecked at the "scarecrow's" head, unaware.

They decided to rest on its hands: look how nice!

And then Rosie snatched them, without thinking twice.

Well, those horrid crows knew that they had been had,

And the scarecrow they'd seen was a woman so mad.

So they pleaded and wept and begged then to Rose,

And you never have seen any sorrier crows.

They promised at once that they'd never come back,

And Rosie, good-hearted, waved them off down the track.

And since then every crow's had the sense not to steal

For it's too hard to tell if a scarecrow is real.

When I created the book I put

a lot of thought and love into it.

I really enjoyed writing my book,

and I hope you enjoyed reading it too.

Adler.sigal@gmail.com

www.ingramcontent.com/pod-product-compliance
Lightning Source LLC
Chambersburg PA
CBHW042011090426
42811CB00015B/1609